When a potter is at work, making perhaps a bowl or a vase, he takes some wet clay on his rotating wheel and, with his fingers, molds it to the shape he wants. The wet clay is said to be *plastic*, which means that it can be readily shaped with pressure. In recent times man has been able to make a considerable number of materials that become plastic when they are heated and can then be shaped into useful articles. We call these new materials plastics.

Using simple diagrams and colorful explanatory illustrations the author discusses the nature of plastics, describes the processes of converting raw materials, and looks at how the plastics industry began with the introduction of celluloid about one hundred years ago.

Finding Out About
SCIENCE
Edited by
Stella Robinson

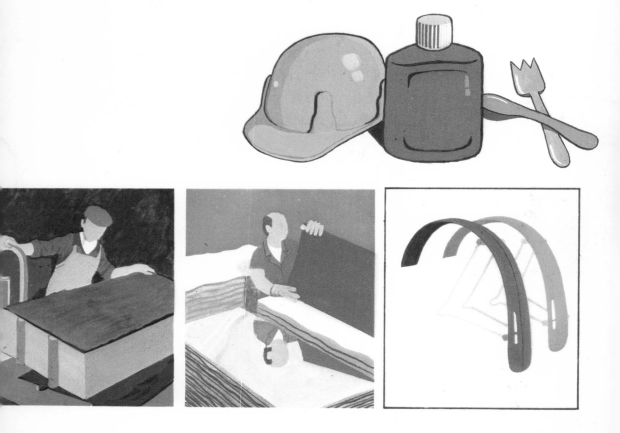

C. P. VALE

PLASTICS

Illustrated by
MICHAEL HUDSON

The John Day Company   New York

Contents

When a potter is at work, making perhaps a bowl or a vase, he takes some wet clay on his rotating wheel and, with his fingers, molds it to the shape he wants. The wet clay is said to be *plastic*, which means that it can be readily shaped with pressure. After it has been shaped or molded, the pot is baked in an oven. It becomes hard and rigid, and the shape is now fixed.

In recent times man has been able to make a considerable number of materials that become plastic when they are heated, and can then be shaped into useful articles. We call these new materials plastics.

6

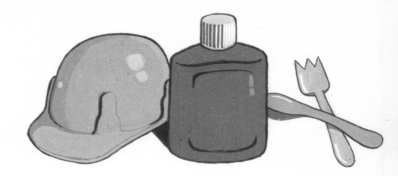

Special molding processes have been developed for them which are much more rapid than that used by the potter. Thus a large number of similar articles can be made in a very short time and, as a result, at much less cost.

In addition to molded objects many other important uses have been found for plastics, as we shall see later on.

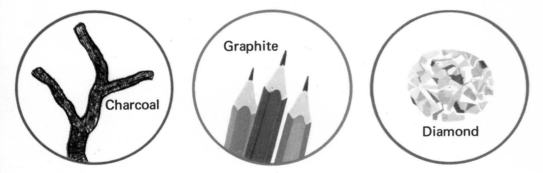

Three different forms of the element carbon: charcoal, obtained by burning wood; graphite – the black lead of pencils; diamond

What are these new materials? We can start to answer this by saying two things that apply to all plastics. First, they are compounds containing the chemical element carbon. Carbon has the remarkable ability to combine with other elements to form many thousands of different substances, many of which are found in plants and animals.

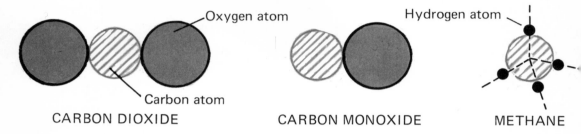

Oxygen atom

Hydrogen atom

Carbon atom

CARBON DIOXIDE

CARBON MONOXIDE

METHANE

Some of these compounds consist of very simple particles or *molecules*. One example is carbon dioxide, which is present in the air we breathe and is the gas that escapes from fizzy drinks. Other carbon compounds, such as sugar, have rather larger and more complicated molecules. Yet another group of materials, found widely in nature, has very large molecules. These

A molecule of cane sugar (sucrose) showing the arrangement of carbon, hydrogen and oxygen atoms

materials include starch, rubber, and natural fibers such as cotton, wool, and silk. Cotton consists almost entirely of an important substance called *cellulose*, which is found in trees and plants. The paper on which this book is printed is made of cellulose that comes mainly from wood.

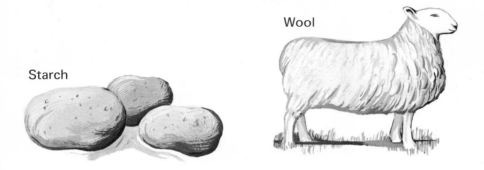

Wool

Rubber

Starch

Three substances, found in nature, having very large molecules

Now the second thing we have to remember about plastics is that they also have very large molecules. In the case of plastics, however, these large molecules are usually built up (or *synthesized*) by man from much simpler chemical compounds, instead of being found in nature. The first of the plastics to be made on a commercial scale, *celluloid* was introduced about a hundred years ago. Many lightweight toys used to be made of this material and our grandmothers often played with celluloid dolls. Celluloid, however, is very inflammable so that nowadays it has been largely replaced by safer plastics.

9

The cotton plant (above) and cotton bolls (right) from which cotton fiber (pure cellulose) is obtained

Paper pulp (cellulose) i obtained mainly from trees.

Celluloid is made from cellulose in the form of paper pulp or cotton fibers. Cellulose, though having very large molecules, is not itself a plastic. When it is heated it breaks down into simpler substances before it can become soft and moldable. On treating with nitric acid, however, it changes into a new substance called *nitrocellulose*. This is separated from the acid, washed with water, dried, and mixed with some camphor. The material thus produced becomes soft when heated. It can then be pressed into blocks from which sheets can be cut, or formed into rods or tubes by processes that will be described later.

Celluloid being pressed into blocks (left); celluloid sheets being polished by placing between heated metal plates (center); bicycle fenders made of celluloid (right)

Toward the end of the nineteenth century a process was invented for obtaining a plastic from skimmed milk. Milk contains a substance called *casein* which has a very large molecule. For the manufacture of casein plastics large vats of skimmed milk are treated at a controlled temperature with a substance called *rennet* (obtained from the stomach of a calf). Casein is produced and is separated, washed, and processed. It was used mostly for making small articles like

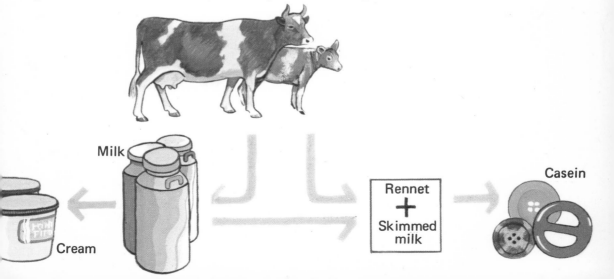

Milk

Cream

Rennet
+
Skimmed
milk

Casein

buttons and buckles, but now it has been largely replaced by new and better plastics.

These two early plastics made use of large molecules already present in nature. The first plastic in which large molecules were built up by man was discovered just before the First World War by a chemist named L. H. Baekeland. It was found that two chemicals, phenol and formaldehyde, acted together to give a product containing large molecules. Phenol (or carbolic acid) is a colorless solid that used to be obtained from coal tar. Nowadays it is obtained more and more from petroleum. Formaldehyde is a gas at ordinary temperatures but it is largely used in the form of a liquid called *formalin*. Formalin is often used in school laboratories for preserving biological specimens.

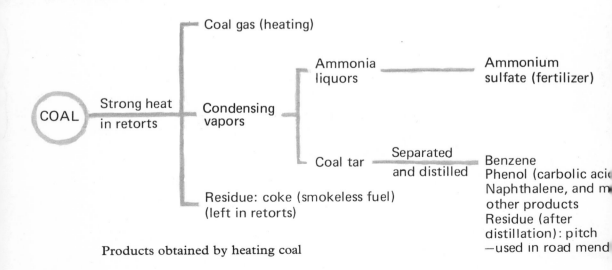

Products obtained by heating coal

When useful articles made from phenol-formaldehyde (or PF) appeared first in the shops they were known by the trade name Bakelite (from the name of their discoverer). Such articles are made from molding materials that contain not only PF but also fibrous material and pigments. Unfortunately PF is dark brown and Bakelite articles could be made only in dark colors (e.g. deep red, brown, black, etc.).

A modern use of Bakelite (PF) moldings: encasing metal parts of steering wheel and column

However, it was later found that if phenol was replaced by another substance called *urea*, this difficulty could be overcome. Urea is a white solid that is made very cheaply. It combines with formaldehyde in a way similar to phenol. The urea-formaldehyde (or UF) is colorless. Thus with colorless fibers, and various pigments, it became possible to make molding materials from which objects could be made in white, cream, and many attractive pale colors.

But UF materials also had drawbacks. Cups, saucers, and plates made from them in these lighter

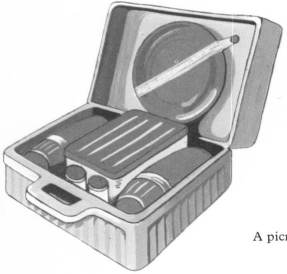

A picnic set made in UF

colors were popular for picnics and other occasional uses. One advantage was that they were much less readily broken than crockery. However, it was found that cups filled with hot tea or coffee absorbed a small amount of water and, with it, any coloring matter present. Thus they became badly stained after a short time if used regularly.

14

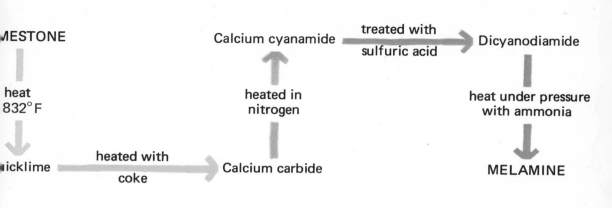

LIMESTONE → heat 832°F → Quicklime → heated with coke → Calcium carbide → heated in nitrogen → Calcium cyanamide → treated with sulfuric acid → Dicyanodiamide → heat under pressure with ammonia → MELAMINE

Diagram showing how melamine is produced

In 1935 it was discovered that another substance, melamine, used with formaldehyde gave a product (MF) which, while being colorless like UF, absorbed far less water and stained far less readily. At that time melamine was an expensive chemical and ways had to be found for making it cheaply. So it was some years before the melamine cups, saucers, and other tableware that

Modern tableware made in MF

we now often see in shops and use in our homes began to appear.

In the thirties entirely new methods were discovered for making very large molecules from small ones and this led to the introduction of such plastics as polyethylene, PVC (polyvinyl chloride) and polystyrene. These are now made and used in very large quantities all over the world and, since the Second World War, have been joined by many new plastics.

We have talked about plastics as a single family of new materials. There are in fact two quite distinct types of plastics. These are the *thermosetting plastics* and the *thermoplastics*. These names, though long, are easy to understand if we remember that *therm* means heat.

The thermosetting plastics, which include PF, UF,

THERMOSETTING PLASTICS	THERMOPLASTICS
Phenol-formaldehyde (PF)	Polyethylene
Urea-formaldehyde (UF)	Polyvinyl chloride (PVC)
Melamine-formaldehyde (MF)	Polystyrene
Alkyds	Polypropylene
Polyesters	Acrylics
Polyurethane	Cellulose acetate
Epoxy	Polyvinyl acetate

MF, and some newer materials that will be mentioned later, behave in the following way: on heating they first become plastic (like putty or the potter's clay) and in this condition they can take on a required shape. On further heating they become hard and rigid and thus retain the shape. They are, as the name suggests, set by heat.

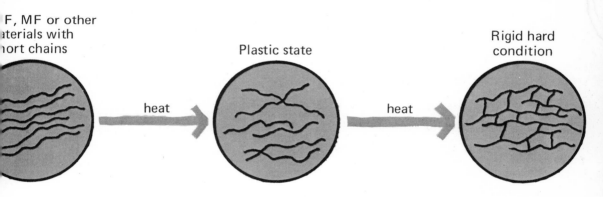

F, MF or other materials with short chains

Plastic state

Rigid hard condition

heat

heat

The thermoplastics, which include polyethylene, PVC, polystyrene, and many others, become plastic on heating, which allows them to be shaped. On cooling they become nonplastic, thus keeping the new shape.

heat

cool

Rigid material

Plastic state

17

By raw materials we mean the chemicals we start with to make plastics. Some of these chemicals are made from cheap and easily obtained substances like air, water, coke, and limestone. Some are obtained from coal tar, which is produced, together with coal gas, when coal is strongly heated. Coal has, however, become a less important source of chemicals for plastics in recent years.

Most raw materials for plastics are obtained from oil or (since there are many different kinds of oil) petroleum. Petroleum is a very complicated mixture of chemicals called *hydrocarbons*. Hydrocarbons are substances containing only the elements hydrogen and carbon. Petroleum, found in different parts of the world, is taken to a refinery. There it is separated into different products and some of the more complex hydrocarbons are broken down into simpler and more useful ones. Valuable products coming from an oil refinery include gasoline, kerosine, and lubricating oils. Also, a number of chemicals are obtained which are used in large quantities for making plastics. The most important of these is the hydrocarbon *ethylene*.

Ethylene under ordinary conditions is a colorless inflammable gas. Its molecules are quite small but are able, under special conditions, to join up one to another rather like a long row of beads. The result is a very long molecule

A modern petroleum refinery ▶

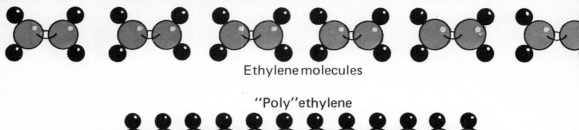

Ethylene molecules

"Poly"ethylene

and the product obtained is a solid thermoplastic, polyethylene, which is often called by its shortened name, polythene. The word *poly*, which we meet so often when we read about plastics, means *many*, and the process by which a great number of small molecules of the same kind join to form a very long molecule is called *polymerization*. Many thermoplastics are made in this way.

From ethylene can be made other chemicals used in making plastics such as vinyl chloride (for making PVC) and styrene (for making polystyrene).

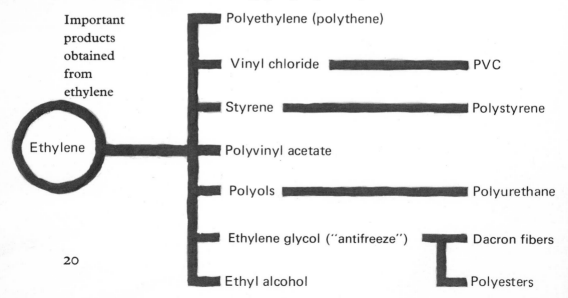

Important products obtained from ethylene

Ethylene

- Polyethylene (polythene)
- Vinyl chloride — PVC
- Styrene — Polystyrene
- Polyvinyl acetate
- Polyols — Polyurethane
- Ethylene glycol ("antifreeze") — Dacron fibers
- Ethyl alcohol — Polyesters

20

For making useful articles, or *moldings*, from plastics, specially prepared *molding powders* or molding compounds are used. These may be in the form of coarse particles rather like sand, or small chips or pellets, or larger pellets made to a required weight and shape. Some molding compounds look something like dough or putty.

A doughy molding composition made from polyester resin

These molding materials may contain not only plastics but also paper fibers, or other fibers like glass or asbestos, which are put in to make the molding stronger. They may also contain dyes or pigments to color it and small amounts of other chemicals to prevent the molding from sticking to the mold or (with thermosetting plastics) to increase the rate at which the material sets.

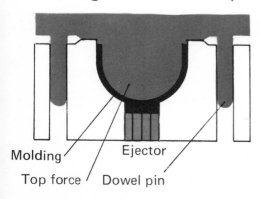

Molding
Top force
Ejector
Dowel pin

A simple compression mold

21

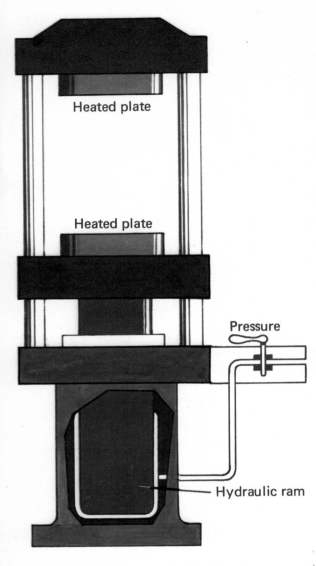

Heated plate

Heated plate

Pressure

Hydraulic ram

Articles are made from thermosetting materials largely by a process called *compression molding*. For this a steel mold is used. A simple mold consists of two parts, an upper and lower, which can be separated. When the two parts of the mold are held together a space remains between them of the shape and size of the article required.

◀ A simple hydraulic press

Removing the hot molding from the mold after compression molding ▶

The mold is fixed to steel plates attached to the upper and lower parts of a hydraulic press (see diagram). The plates are heated and the heat is conducted to the

mold which, in turn, heats up to the required temperature (about 300 °F). To make a molding, the molding material is weighed out. The press is opened, separating the mold parts. The powder is placed in the lower part and the press then closed. The molding material heats up, becomes plastic, and, with the pressure on it, flows to fill the space between the parts of the mold. After

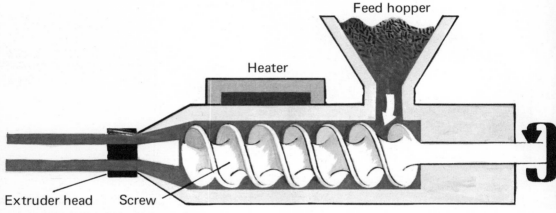

Feed hopper

Heater

Extruder head   Screw

The principle of extrusion

allowing time for the material to set, the pressure is taken off. The press then opens and the molded article—quite hot but hard and rigid—is taken out.

Several methods are used for making useful articles from thermoplastics. One method, for making long, continuous objects like curtain rods, garden hoses, or guttering for the roofs of buildings, is called *extrusion*. Small pellets of the material are fed from a container into one end of a long horizontal steel tube inside which a screw turns. The tube is heated and the material soon becomes plastic. It is forced along the tube by the screw and through a hole at the far end. It comes out, still plastic, as a continuous length with a shape which depends on the shape of the hole, and is quickly cooled with a jet of air or by cold water to make it nonplastic and keep its shape.

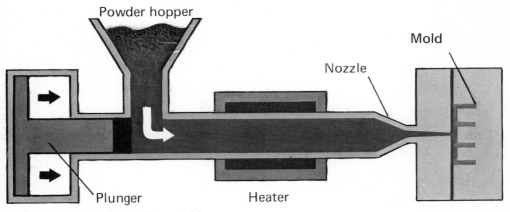

The principle of injection molding

Useful objects are also made by a process called *injection molding*. The material, as in extrusion, is fed to a heated tube where it becomes plastic. It is then pushed by a plunger or a screw through a nozzle into a closed cold mold. After a short time to allow the material to cool down and become rigid, the mold is opened and the finished article is taken out. The mold is then closed and the procedure repeated.

The principle of blow molding

Hollow articles like bottles are made by a process called *blow molding*. An extrusion machine is used to produce a continuous tube of material. While the tube is still hot and plastic a cold mold closes around part of it and a jet of cold air is blown through the tube forcing it against the surface of the mold and shaping it. The material quickly cools, becoming nonplastic, and on opening the mold the finished article falls out.

There are now many different sorts of plastics of both the thermosetting and thermoplastic types. These differ in price and in properties, but some things can be said about molded plastics that are true of all of them.

First, they are much lighter in weight than most metals. Next, they can be colored, and many of them can be obtained in a wide range of colors. They are not corroded by moist air as many metals are—particularly iron and

The weight in grams of one cubic inch of well-known materials in comparison with some plastics

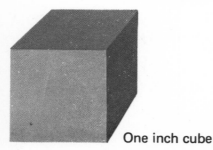

One inch cube

Material	Weight	Material	Weight
Steel	128	Polythene	15-16
Brass	138	PVC	23
Gold	316	Polystyrene	17
Lead	185	Celluloid	22
Aluminum	44	UF	25
Marble	44	Nylon	18-19
Wood (Oak)	12	Acrylic	20

steel, which readily rust. Again, while metals are very good conductors of electricity, plastics are electrical insulators and do not conduct electricity. They find many uses in electrical equipment for this reason. Finally, and also unlike metals, they are poor conductors of heat and so are useful for such purposes as handles for cooking utensils.

A good way of appreciating how much plastic moldings are used is to look around your own home, taking note of any molded objects you see, and try to imagine what would happen if all plastics suddenly disappeared. You will notice electric plugs, sockets, and adapters; and

The plastic handle, being a poor conductor of heat, allows a heated metal rod to be held in the hand

possibly knobs and push buttons on your radio and TV sets. In the kitchen you may have cups, saucers, and plates molded in MF; a polythene dishpan or bucket; a teakettle, saucepan, or frying pan with a plastic handle. If you look inside your refrigerator or washing machine, you will find plastic moldings, and if you have a fan in the kitchen for sucking out fumes this too may very well be made largely of plastic parts. So will be your telephone and your father's electric shaver. But an even closer look will show that quite common objects that we rarely give a thought to are plastic moldings also: the screw cap of an ink bottle, the cap of a

toothpaste tube, bottles containing detergents and bleaches, bottles containing cosmetics, buttons, and many other minor items. And a glance in your toy cupboard will remind you how many toys are made from plastics or have plastic parts.

But moldings are only one of a number of ways in which plastics are used. You are probably familiar with Formica, a material in sheet form that is used to cover tables and working spaces in kitchens. This type of sheet, which has an attractive color and appearance as well as being hard, smooth, and easy to clean, is a *laminate*. Formica is the trade name used by one producer, but there are many other equally good laminates.

The word *lamina* means a thin layer and laminates are made by combining thin layers of material to form a strong sheet.

To make a plastic laminate, paper sheet is soaked in a solution containing a thermosetting resin. The sheet is dried in an oven, the resin being left behind on the paper. Layers of paper containing the plastic resin are placed on top of each other to form a pile which is then put between a pair of polished steel plates. The whole is then placed in a hydraulic press fitted with heated plates (as in compression molding) and the press closed. The resin becomes plastic, flows, and then sets, forming a strong, rigid sheet.

In making the decorative laminates used in kitchens, the next-to-the-top layer in the pile is made from a paper printed with the required design and contains MF. Above this is placed a very thin layer of paper, also containing

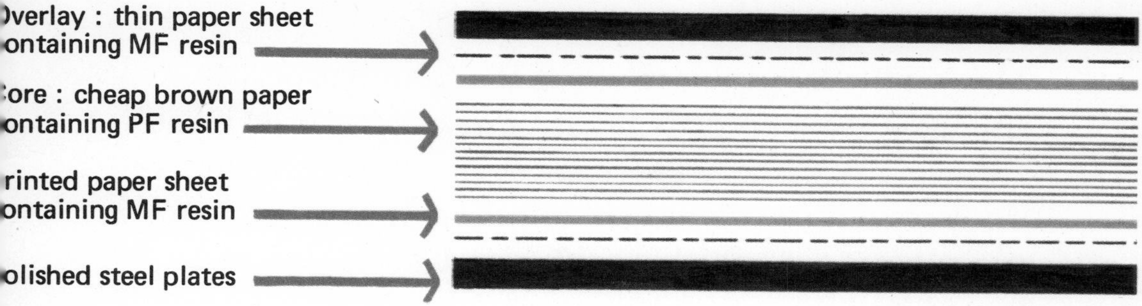

Overlay : thin paper sheet
containing MF resin →

Core : cheap brown paper
containing PF resin →

Printed paper sheet
containing MF resin →

Polished steel plates →

MF. This acts as a transparent covering protecting the
design underneath.

Though paper is most often used, cotton fabric, glass
cloth, and other sheet materials are sometimes used for
making laminates. Thin laminates made with PF and MF
resins are used as electrical insulators.

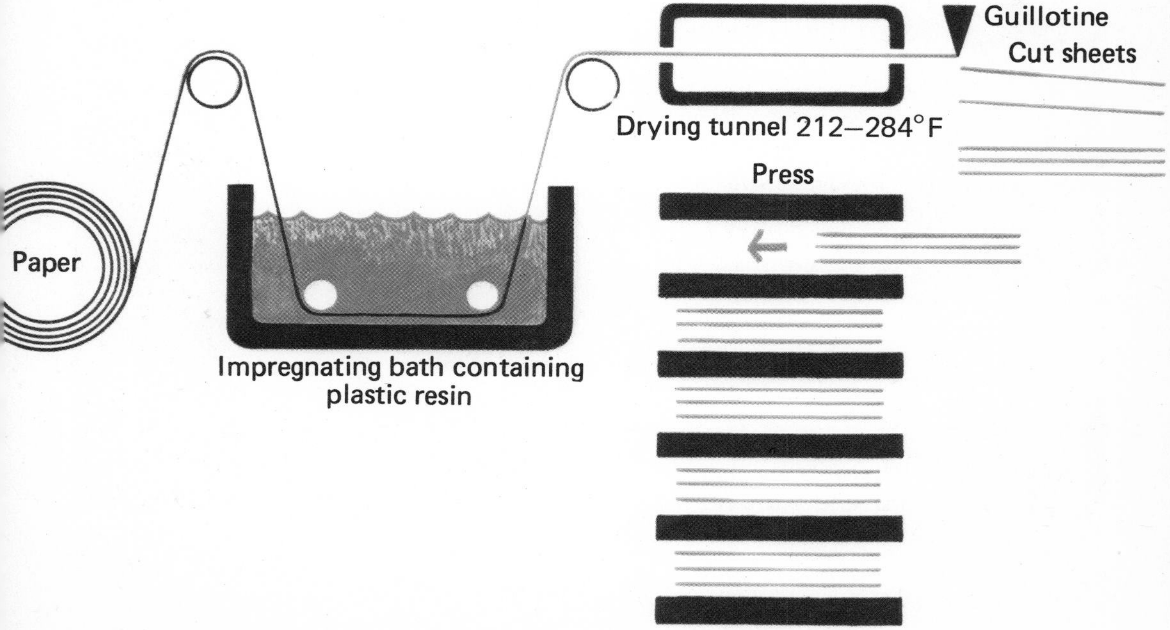

Paper

Impregnating bath containing
plastic resin

Drying tunnel 212—284°F

Guillotine
Cut sheets

Press

Many quite large objects are made from plastics strengthened with glass fibers. The plastics used mostly are called *polyesters*. These are sticky liquids rather like molasses but usually nearly colorless. If small amounts of two substances, called a *catalyst* and a *promoter*, are stirred into them nothing seems to happen for a time. Then suddenly the liquid turns into a jelly, becomes quite hot, and finally sets to a hard, solid mass.

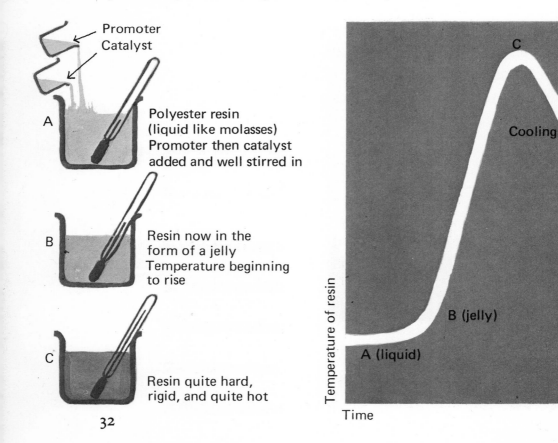

Promoter
Catalyst

A Polyester resin
(liquid like molasses)
Promoter then catalyst
added and well stirred in

B Resin now in the
form of a jelly
Temperature beginning
to rise

C Resin quite hard,
rigid, and quite hot

C

Cooling

Temperature of resin

B (jelly)

A (liquid)

Time

If the polyester, containing catalyst and promoter, is brushed on so as to soak into sheets of glass fiber or glass cloth placed in a mold, on setting a very strong product is obtained. By putting on further layers of glass and polyester an object can be built up to any thickness.

Making a boat using sheets of glass fiber and polyester resin. The glass fiber sheets are laid on a mold and polyester resin (containing catalyst and promoter) is brushed or rolled into the surface. The resin sets after a short time and further layers of glass and resin can be applied until the required thickness is obtained.

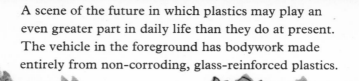

A scene of the future in which plastics may play an even greater part in daily life than they do at present. The vehicle in the foreground has bodywork made entirely from non-corroding, glass-reinforced plastics.

Boats, garden pools, storage tanks, chimney stacks and even church spires can be made with these materials. Light in weight and strong, they do not corrode, and if damaged can be easily repaired with more glass and polyester. Pigments and other substances are often added to the polyester to give color to the object made and make it opaque. However, sheets made from glass fibers and some polyesters are almost completely transparent and are used as roofing material in factories, garages, swimming pools, and other buildings, allowing light to enter freely.

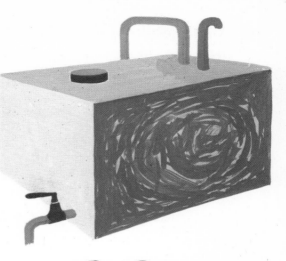

An adhesive or glue is a substance used to bond two objects together. Animal glues made from bones and skins; glues and gums made from starch obtained from potatoes and cereals; and adhesives made from casein obtained from milk have been known and used for many years.

These older glues have two drawbacks. The number of different materials they can stick together is limited. Also they tend to be affected by moisture, bacteria, and molds so that the glue joint formed is not very lasting, particularly in warm and moist surroundings.

Pieces of wood glued together with a casein glue (left) and a UF resin adhesive (right) showing the result of soaking for several hours in water

With the development of plastics a number of new adhesives made from plastic resins have been introduced. These not only give stronger and more permanent joints, but with the great variety of different plastics it is now possible to stick almost any material to any other. Thus, for example, with adhesives made from *epoxy* resins (plastics of the thermosetting type) it is possible to stick metal to metal, metal to glass, metal to plastic, and many other combinations.

Plywood is nowadays made using UF and PF adhesives. A thin layer of the adhesive is coated on to sheets of wood (veneers) which are then assembled so that the grain of each sheet is at right angles to that of the one next to it, and then placed in a heated hydraulic press until the adhesive has thermoset. A bond stronger than the wood itself is formed.

Another useful material is chipboard. This is made by coating small chips or flakes of wood with a UF adhesive and then pressing the pieces together in special molds in a heated press.

The arrangement of veneers in plywood (above).
If you have a scrap of plywood try carefully prying
apart the layers with a penknife. A clean separation
of the veneers is almost impossible to achieve
because the adhesive bond is stronger than the wood itself.

A paint has three important parts: a pigment, a hard transparent resin, and a solvent. The pigment gives color and hides the surface underneath. The resin holds the pigment in place and protects it. The solvent dissolves the resin, allows it to flow out forming a smooth surface, and then evaporates.

In most paints nowadays the resin part is a plastic material. Paints used for house decoration mostly contain plastic resins called *alkyds*.

Smooth hard resin surface   Solvent evaporating   Pigment particles embedded in hardened resin

SUBSTRATE

The enamels that give hard, glossy, and weather-proof finishes on cars and bicycles usually contain a mixture of an alkyd and an MF resin. The enamels are sprayed on to give a smooth finish. The solvent evaporates off, and the resin is thermoset by passing through an oven at about 250 °F.

Enamels containing thermosetting plastic resins (UF, MF and alkyds) are used for giving hard protective coatings, for example to cars and tricycles

38

Thermoplastics can be used in *lacquers*, which dry hard without heat. Touching-up paints for covering scratches on cars, for example, contain nitrocellulose in a solvent. After applying, the solvent quickly evaporates, leaving a dry film in about 10 to 15 minutes. Clear lacquers of this type, containing no pigment, are used for putting transparent and glossy coats on woodwork and other materials.

Many thermoplastics are made into thin films and sheets. Flexible sheets of PVC are used as curtaining, and for making light, pack-away raincoats. Transparent, rigid sheets, known by the trade name Perspex, are sometimes used as material for windows instead of glass. The most important use for plastic films and sheets, however, is for packaging goods.

A strong, waterproof PVC coat

Walking around a supermarket, you will find many foods wrapped in clear film so that they can be seen yet are protected from human hands. Items of clothing are similarly wrapped.

Films of polythene and PVC are used in the form of sacks to hold potatoes, fertilizers, and other materials. They are quite strong and waterproof.

Sheets of polythene are often used to surround partly

Packaging with polyethylene film

Polythene film used to protect crops

Plastic resins (usually UF or MF) introduced in small quantities into paper make it strong when thoroughly soaked with water. Wet-strength paper is used for paper towels. A piece of ordinary paper (newspaper or toilet tissue) on soaking with water has very little strength and readily shreds up when rubbed between the fingers. A similar piece of wet-strength paper (paper toweling) on soaking with water remains quite strong.

erected buildings allowing the builders to work in wet and windy conditions. They also find many uses in farming.

There are a number of ways by which films and sheet are made, but perhaps the most important is extrusion. The thermoplastic material is extruded to give a continuous length of tube. A jet of air blown through the tube causes it to expand considerably, like a balloon being

Nip rollers

Film bubble

Cooling ring

Extruder

Inflation air

Wind up

blown up. The thin and, by now, nonplastic sheet is led upward between rollers and wound up as a continuous double sheet. This can be cut into lengths later and one end of each length completely sealed by heat to make transparent bags.

Making film by extrusion and blowing ▶

◀ Diagram to show how this plant operates

Yet another form in which plastics are used is that of solid foams. These can be flexible like a sponge, or quite rigid yet very light in weight.

Foams are often made by introducing into a plastic material a chemical called a *blowing agent*. This on heating either turns into a vapor or releases a gas. The gas causes the material in the plastic state to expand and fills

it with bubbles. The material then sets, or becomes nonplastic by cooling, before the bubbles can escape.

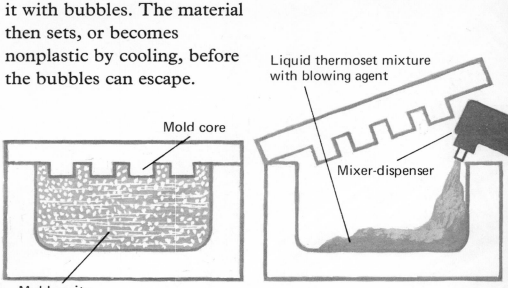

Liquid thermoset mixture with blowing agent

Mold core

Mixer-dispenser

Mold cavity

Flexible foams made from a thermosetting plastic called *polyurethane* are now very much used in cushioning and in upholstery. They are also used as sponges, on paint rollers, and around windows to keep out drafts.

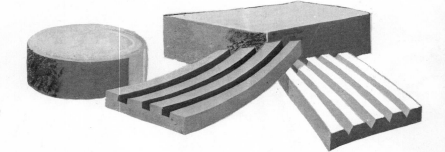

All plastic foams are very good heat insulators. Thus thin sheets of flexible foam used as linings inside coats, or in slippers, keep in the heat of the body and are warm and comfortable.

Rigid foams are also used for heat insulation. Foamed polystyrene ceiling tiles are both attractive in appearance and reduce heat losses from a room. Normally a house is built with an inner and an outer wall between which is left a cavity. If this cavity is filled with a rigid plastic

foam the amount of heat lost from a house is considerably reduced, as are fuel bills. Special machines can be brought to the site and the plastic foam pumped into the wall cavities and set on the spot.

Rigid foams are beginning to replace wood in the manufacture of furniture. Both rigid and flexible foams are used for packaging delicate instruments and fragile objects. Rigid foams pumped into free spaces in boats give

A possible future use for plastic fo (UF). Thick beds of foam formed the end of airport runways rapidl arrest the movement of aircraft wl have accidentally gone beyond the runway

them added buoyancy and reduce any likelihood of sinking.

In this book it has been possible to mention only a few of the many ways in which these recently developed materials called plastics are made and used. New materials, new methods of shaping these materials, and new uses are being sought for and discovered each year.

It is not too early to say that plastics, materials entirely devised by man, are now as important in our modern world as the older and traditional materials wood, metal, and stone, which have been used by man for many centuries.

Some of the new words you have read in this book:

Alkyds—Man-made resins used for making household paints.
Blowing agent—A chemical introduced into a plastic which, by giving off a gas while the plastic is setting, turns it into a foam.
Blow molding—A method of shaping plastics used in making bottles.
Casein—A substance, found in milk, used to make one of the earliest plastics.
Catalyst—A substance which starts or speeds up a chemical process.
Celluloid—The first commercial plastic made from nitrocellulose and camphor.
Cellulose—The material plants are mostly made of, used for making paper and plastics.
Compression molding—A method of shaping thermosetting plastics in a mold with heat and pressure.
Epoxy—A thermosetting plastic used mainly as a strong adhesive.
Ethylene—A colorless gas from which many plastics are made.
Extrusion—Squeezing a melted thermoplastic through a hole to make a rod or tube.
Formalin—A solution of "formaldehyde" used in the production of plastics.
Hydrocarbon—A chemical made from hydrogen and carbon.
Injection molding—Forming plastics by forcing molten plastic into a mold.
Lacquers—Solutions of a resin which applied to an object give it a protective coat.
Lamina—A thin, flat sheet of material.
Laminate—A sheetlike material made from sheets of paper or fabric and plastic combined together using heat and pressure.
Molecule—The smallest unit of a chemical substance that can exist.
Molding powders—Plastics in powder form from which shapes are molded.
Moldings—Articles made from plastics by a molding process.
Nitrocellulose—A substance made by reacting cellulose with nitric acid.
Plastic (adjective)—The property of a material that allows it to be shaped.
Poly-—A prefix that means "many."
Polyester—A plastic resin mostly used in combination with glass fibers to form strong objects.
Polymerization—A process by which small molecules link together to form very large molecules.
Polyurethane—A plastic used in making plastic foams and in paints.
Promoter—A substance which increases the activity of a catalyst.
Rennet—A substance which added to milk causes casein to separate.
Synthesized—Built up from simple chemicals.
Therm-—A prefix meaning "heat."
Thermoplastics—Materials that become plastic on heating and nonplastic on cooling.
Thermosetting plastics—Materials that become plastic on heating, and on further heating become nonplastic.
Urea—A colorless chemical made from ammonia and carbon dioxide.

48

Printed in Great Britain